Poems and Illustrations
by
**Nancy Arbuthnot**

To order additional copies of this book, contact:
Xlibris
844-714-8691
www.Xlibris.com
Orders@Xlibris.com

ISBN:      Softcover      978-1-6641-9482-3
              EBook          978-1-6641-9483-0

Print information available on the last page

Rev. date: 02/24/2022

For Zoe—

dear first grandchild, born during my art residency at Catoctin Mountain Park, who bestowed upon me the letter Z—

For the Catoctin park rangers, staff and visitors

And for the pupils of Crow Agency Public School who participated in my poet-in-the-schools workshops in Montana in 1981 and gave me, forty years later, the title for this book. From the poem by one young student:

### Remember Me Singing

*Remember me singing in the moonlight*
*when the blue star lights up in the sky*
*when the stones turn blue and leaves*
*turn green and the river is blue*
*and the moon is still*

The Catoctin Forest Alliance (CFA) is a friends' group to Catoctin Mountain Park and adjacent Cunningham Falls State Park whose mission is to preserve and promote the health of the Catoctin Mountain forest for the enjoyment of present and future generations. Its programs focus on educating both children and adults to be powerful stewards and champions of the environment in this special place. Our group has sponsored the Artist-in-Residence (AIR) program since 2010 and has attracted artists from all over the US for 2-3 week residencies. During their time in the parks, the artists create art inspired by the forest.

Nancy Arbuthnot was our artist for 2020 and 2021, chosen by the jury panel for her clarity of watercolor composition and her accompanying haiku poems. Although she was not able to be in residence in Catoctin Mountain Park for the 2020 residency due to COVID, she visited the park numerous times and created virtual programs that were used by local school children to increase their appreciation of nature and artistic creativity.

Because Nancy did not have the resident experience in 2020, we invited her back in May 2021. While living in an historic cabin in the park for three weeks, she hiked and biked the trails, researched the flora and fauna and created art that was inspired by her surroundings. Her final project is this ABC book of things Catoctin--a watercolor painting for each letter of the alphabet with an accompanying poem inspired by lists of favorite things provided by visitors, volunteers, staff and friends of the park.

# I: Catoctin Mountain Park

Catoctin Mountain Park, part of the National Park System of the United States, is part of the forested Catoctin Mountain ridge-range that forms the northeastern rampart of the Blue Ridge Mountains in the Appalachian Mountains System. It is located in north-central Maryland, approximately 70 miles northwest of both Baltimore and Washington, DC. The name "Catoctin," which may derive from the Kittoctons, an American Indian group which once lived between the mountain and the Potomac River, also refers to a residual hill or ridge that rises above a peneplain (a low-relief plain formed by protracted erosion) and preserves on its summit a remnant of an older peneplain.

The park got its start during the Great Depression of the 1930s as a place for people to reconnect with nature. In one small location, Catoctin's diverse natural and cultural resources reflect much of the early fabric of our country and provide telling vignettes of our nation's history. During the Archaic Period (8000 to 1200 BCE) through the Woodland Period (1200 BCE to 1600 CE), but most actively between 200 and 900 CE, Native Americans quarried rhyolite here for the production of tools, some now on display at the Visitor Center. From the 17th to the early 20th centuries small industries worked by European immigrants and free and enslaved blacks--farming, milling timber, and whiskey production--thrived in the area, and remnants of old roads, stone walls, cellar holes, sawmill races and a whiskey still are visible. A significant charcoal enterprise of woodcutters and charcoal makers consumed timber from 11,000 acres

The 20th century brought new uses to the land. In the 1930s, President Roosevelt founded a national system of Recreational Demonstration Areas near urban centers for recreational use of city dwellers, including the Catoctin RDA, where workers with the Works Progress Administration (WPA) and the Civilian Conservation Corps (CCC) built the historic chestnut logs cabins and other structures still used today. During World War II, Roosevelt created the nation's first official national security agency, the Office of Strategic Services (predecessor to the CIA), using Catoctin lands and facilities for the training of recruits. In 1954, the RDA lands were transferred to the National Park Service, and in 1960, President Johnson established our nation's first Job Corps Center at Catoctin. All these programs offer tangible reminders of how our government strengthens our nation's security, economy and social fabric. Today Catoctin Mountain Park remains true to its recreational origins, and takes on new significance as new generations discover not only the glories of jewel-like spring flowers, fiery autumn leaves and rocky trails along streams or uphill to spectacular valley vistas, but the human history of the land as well.

Through its Artist-In-Residence (AIR) program, Catoctin Mountain Park supports the lively tradition of artists in America's national parks, where artists have played a vital role in preserving our nation's natural treasures. The first suggestion of a "nation's park," in fact, came from artist George Catlin in 1832, and since the late 19th century, when the Hudson River School painters captured the majestic views of our nation's western parks, artists have created art in national parks. Their creations in turn help with the park system's mission of conservation and enjoyment. Co-sponsored with the Catoctin Forest Alliance, Catoctin Mountain Park offers

As artist-in-residence at Catoctin Mountain Park for three weeks in May, 2021, I fulfilled a life-long dream of living in a log cabin in the woods and making art all day long. From the beginning of my residency I had planned a collection of poems and illustrations of things animal and vegetable, and as my knowledge of the park grew—and my knowledge of history and science expanded too--I added representative samples of the geologic and human history in the park as well. This book, *Remember Me Singing: A Catoctin Mountain Alphabet*, is the result.

During those early-spring days at Catoctin, I roamed freely in sun and rain, eventually hiking all 25 miles of trails (and accumulating more miles with hikes in the adjoining Cunningham Falls State Park). Alone on the mountain except for occasional husband-visits and chats with rangers and the occasional hiker, and without cell phone reception or internet access and with no transportation other than my feet and my son's old childhood bicycle, I usually stayed close to Camp Greentop, where I was housed at Good Luck Lodge. I explored the woods and meadows and wetlands around the cabins at Greentop and followed the horse trail across Park Road through Chestnut Picnic Grove and down across Manahan Road. I worked fifteen or sixteen or seventeen hours a day, hiking, sketching, painting, reading, writing. Often I'd focus on the same intimate but daily-changing scenes: the striped spathe of the jack-in-the-pulpit outside my front door that turned from green to purple; the squiggling tadpoles in the pond that grew legs, lost tails, and hopped onto lily pads; the nestlings under the eaves of a vacant

In my poems, in contrast, I sought to convey interesting and evocative scientific details. By echoing images, subjects, words and themes--the ephemerality of flowers, for example, or the variety of human interactions with the land--I attempt to draw the individual poems and illustrations into a whole, a long illustrated poem about the park. Of course, the book can only begin to skim the surface of the wealth that Catoctin offers. But I hope it will inspire further exploration, outside in nature and inside--in the library, in the cyber-space of the world-wide-web, and in your own minds--as you find your own favorite things to make Catoctin Mountain Park a part of you.

Nancy Arbuthnot, Washington, DC
December 2021

on this easternmost rampart
of the Appalachian Blue Ridge:

Adirondack shelters
acorns from oaks
ants in the cabin of the artist-in-residence
(a talk with the park biologist
*Let's let them live*)—

African American cemetery
at the foot of the mountain
unquiet graves of free blacks and enslaved
names re-discovered in old documents and letters
      Ann, Annenise, Arnold, Archibald
      Daniel, David, Elias, Estor
      Ezekial, Old Hanna, Hesekiah
      Old Jack, Maria, Nicholas, Romeo
      Wally, Yellow Girl, Zacharia
say the names, one and all, call the restless souls back--

bear nuzzling bear corn
in the woods near Brown's farm

bats nestling beneath bark
of shagbark hickories

box turtle, *Terrapene carolina*
stepping through grass, head lifted to sun

bluebird at Blue Ridge Summit Vista
gurgling its feeding song, *tu-a-wee, tu-a-wee*

Blue Blazes Whiskey Trail
gunshots still echoing--

Catoctin Mountain Park:

canopy of trees
sweet columbine
cellar-holes of once-farm homes
Owens Creek Campground
Chimney Rock Trail

*Castanea dentata*, American Chestnut
ancient tree of the vast Eastern forest
once-storied giants
used to fuel the Catoctin Furnace
and to build WPA cabins
struck with blight, gone--

among wineberry brambles
arcing toward earth

a doe
nudging her mottled fawn up

dogwood, *Cornus florida*
lifting silk petals
a lacy white mist
in just-greening woods--

environment
ecology
forest ecosystem of plants, animals
and things living and non-living (soil,
water, air)

spring ephemerals
wildflowers blooming briefly
before trees leaf out

bushy-tailed Eastern fox squirrel, *Scirius niger*
with whiskery touch-receptors
on forearms, chin, nose
and above and below each eye
identifying danger
and sustenance
such as seeds from oaks, walnuts, pines—

fern fronds unfurling

sweet musty fox grape
with spiraling vines

*Pseudacris crucifers,* spring's first frogs
peeping in ponds

daisy fleabane, *Erigeron strigosus*
yellow center ringed by white petal-rays

delicate, hardy, fleeting
pointing the way--

ghost plant, *Monotropa uniflora*
without chlorophyll, with no need of sun
pale, glowing, in deep forest shade

great horned owl
at Greentop high on a snag
white scapular feathers aglow
before its silent strike

Catoctin Greenstone
metamorphic rock unique to the mountain
transformed 500 million years ago
from igneous lava, stillness
still flowing, shifting our minds
from impatient human to slow geologic time--

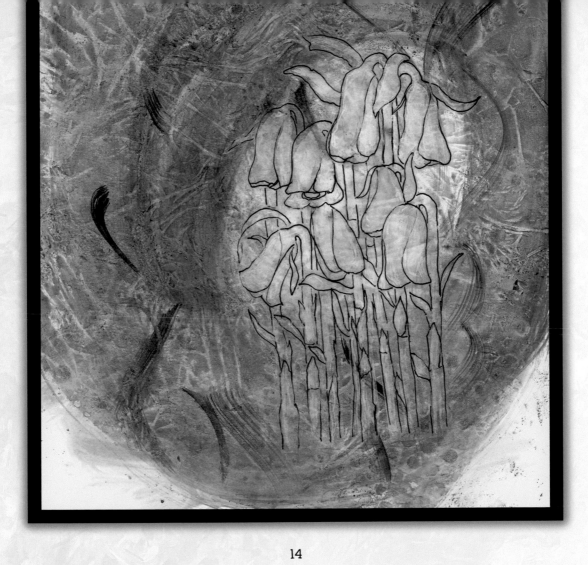

14

hepatica
small buttercup
blooming pink, white, blue, purple
spring into summer

Hog Rock
flat metabasalt outcropping
where mountain farm pigs lounged
after feasting on hickory nuts
where today's hikers pause

habitat
environment where an organism can find
food, water, cover
and space to survive--

hidden things
things camouflaged
leaf bugs, walking sticks
rattlesnakes, whiskey stills--

iron industry of the mountain
worked by European immigrants and their descendants
and enslaved Africans and their descendants--

iron ore miners and wood cutters
haulers and colliers
founders who operated the furnace
and molders who cast pig iron
into stoves, pots, firescreens, cannonballs

the Iron Master
and the Iron Master's Mansion
crumbled to ruins

the Isabella Stack
named for the wife
sturdily standing--

bluejay
with its joy of acorns
that helped spread oak forests across America
and a noisy *jay jay jay*
that warns of danger


Jack-in-the-pulpit, *Arisaema tripyllum*
woodland perennial
with striped hood-like spathe
arching over a spadex of tiny flowers


and roots, munched by deer
that blister human skin
and berries devoured by turkey and woodthrush
that burn human mouths and throats—

20

Kittoctins:
fabled Woodland wanderers
first human visitors
who quarried rhyolite here
gave the mountain its name
left behind tools and projectile points
now on exhibit
once traded widely across the mid-Atlantic

standing before this lithic display
we from the Anthropocene
imagine the makers
chipping stone against stone
faces ghostly in the stream--

22

lichen:
among earth's oldest inhabitants
a complex partnership
between alga and fungus

in forms foliose, fruticose, crustose
squamulose or leprose
they absorb carbon and sulfur
and heavy metals such as arsenic and lead
reducing pollution

and with arms flat and leafy
shrubby and tufted
tightly crusted
or scaly and powdery
envelope wood, rock, dirt
and decompose trees, houses, gravestones
preparing new soils for new life--

in early May
long before monarchs return
to nectar on milkweed
or mountain laurel blooms white and pink and deep-rose
even before the Mayapple, *Podophyllum peltatum*
blossoms

the morel mushroom, *Morchella esculenta*
delectable fungus
sometimes called *mirkle* (for *miracle*)
pushes through dirt and leaf-detritus

at Misty Mount, off Manahan Road
carrying mesh bags the foragers arrive
spread the spores among leaves and millipedes
so that the mushrooms may roam
wider over the mountain--

26

nymphs of caddisfly, mayfly, stonefly
newt


nocturnal, rarely seen in the light
Northern Copperhead
with keeled scales hourglass-patterned
and triangular head
with vertical pupils in coppery eyes


new moon
night sky
North Star *Polaris* a guide
oh follow the Drinking Gourd--

28

OSS recruits, first official spies
from the Office of Strategic Services
America's first centralized intelligence agency
who under false names and identities
shouldered backpacks to tight-rope across Owen's Creek
(often ending up wet)
and learned to fire rifles and to stab with bayonets--

now at Owen's Creek Campground
a Baltimore Oriole flashes black and orange
into green leaves
and at night a barred owl, *Strix varia*
lures campers to sleep
*who cooks for you, who cooks for you all--*

Park Central Road:

light plash and tumble
of water over rocks

purple-fringed orchids
picnics in dappled light

musical *fee-be fee-be*
*Sayornis phoebe* perched on a branch
pumping its tail

peace of the mountain singing
peace in the heart--

quartzite outcroppings of Chimney Rock, Wolf Rock
once-igneous basalt changed over eons
by earth's suppressions, upheavals--


White oak, *Quercas alba*
(for the whitish undersides of its leaves)
predominant hardwood of the eastern forests
used for railroad ties, fence posts
whiskey barrels, caskets--


oh to be as strong as the white oak
as quiet as quartzite--

34

remnants and relics:
roads built by farmers and woodhaulers
races for channeling stream-water to power sawmills
rhyolite knappings

still thriving:
red Canada lily, *Lilium canadense*
edible fruit
for the first foragers of this land--

36

spring peeper
five-lined skink
scarlet tanager
snapping turtle
sassafras
shagbark hickory
spicebush
sugar maple


seed
seedpod
seedling
sapling
standing tree
snag
stump, fallen log
soil
life cycle--

wild turkey trailed by a dozen poults
tulip poplar with leaves like little cat faces

brook trout, *Salvelinus fontinalis*
leaping for flies in Big Hunting Creek

timber rattler, coiled
at Thurmont Vista--

understory
the vegetative layer
(in the language of forest ecology)
of fungi, mosses, lichens, seedlings, saplings
shrubs and bushes
between forest floor and tree canopy

underground dens, nests, burrows
of fox, chipmunk, squirrel
bees, wasp, yellow jackets
cicada larvae aerating the soil
as they shovel upward to emerge after years
ever so briefly

underground roots
looping over and under in cross-border
tree-to-tree communication
erupting above ground

underground railroad
stony the road
trailing the Catoctin range
north to freedom--

family *Violaceae*:
the purple, white and yellow flowers
savory spring nourishment for turkeys and fritillaries
the later seed husks
oily rich food for ants


veery, plump forest thrush,
forager of invertebrates, peering
moving, peering, repeating
and at dusk and dawn releasing
over this vista of Maryland piedmont farms and towns
its downward-spiraling cascade
of song--

WPA
WWII's Ritchey boys
and other locals
who helped lead our country to victory

Wolf Rock
wolf spiders
wineberry
Whiskey Trail
whippoorwills
house wrens
woodpeckers
white-tailed deer

waterfalls on the Atlantic fall line:
across the piedmont's hard metamorphosed terrain
and the sandy outwash of the coastal plain
waters tumbling, rippling
winding to the sea--

46

eXoskeletons
of red-eyed Brood X-ers, *Magicicada septendecim*
seventeen-year cicadas
sipping xylem from tree roots
through straw-like beaks
growing and molting, tunneling up
when the soil warms to 64 degrees
males vibrating tymbals
(thin membranes along the hollow abdomens)
and females within an hour of mating
laying hundreds of eggs
which will hatch and burrow underground
for another seventeen years
then climb upwards to sing and mate
food for birds
fertilizer for the earth--

48

yarrow
medicinal "wound wort"
blood-stanching perennial

yellow petals of black-eyed susans

yellowhammer
nickname for the northern flicker

yellow-shafted woodpecker
gold underwings flashing
in undulating, roller-coaster flight

tiger swallowtail, *Papilio glaucus*
yellow wings edged black

yellow triangle blaze of the Deerfield Nature Trail
yellow rectangle blaze
of the Blue Ridge Summit/Hog Rock/Visitor Center trail
steep, rocky, gently sloping, looping
hikers back to their beginning--

50

zooplankton, from Greek *zoon* for "animal"
and *plankto*, "wanderer":


organisms usually microscopic
adrift or self-propelling through water
often ascending towards the surface at sunset
descending by sunrise to lower depths
in diurnal vertical migrations


Zoe, Greek for "life"
the divine life of the gods:


child newborn
from whatever depths you have come
from what life before
with grace and wonder may you wander these shores--

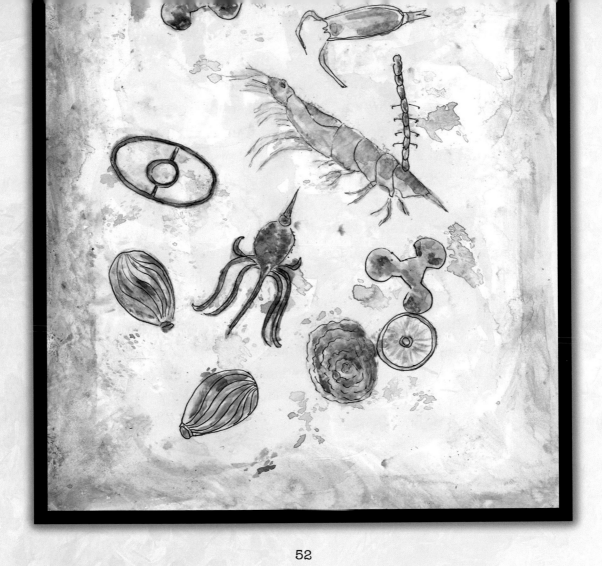

Heartfelt thanks for those who gave me the opportunity to live and work in Catoctin Mountain Park as the 2021 Artist-in-Residence: first, to the National Park Service for creating the AIR program and CMP (Catoctin Mountain Park) and the CFA (Catoctin Forest Alliance) for co-sponsoring the Catoctin AIR program. Special thanks to CMP Superintendent Rick Slade for his support; Ranger Carrie Andresen-Strawn, who shepherded me through all aspects of my residency and gently nudged me through the first amorphous concepts of a project to its completion, and Linda Sundergill, CFA chair of the AIR program, whose team selected me as the CMP artist for both 2020 (during Covid closures) and 2021, and who visited with coffee, books and other friends of the park whose stories of Catoctin enriched my understanding. Thanks to other park rangers and staff who helped make my residency so memorable, including Ranger Conrad Pavlin, who created a video of me at work for the CMP website and provided the model drawing of the timber rattlesnake; Ranger Amy King, who scanned and prepared prints of my images and poems; Becky Loncosky, Park Biologist, who provided me with information about ants and frogs and phoebes and wineberries as well as a microscope to search for microorganisms; and Chief Darling and the US Park Police staff who keep vigilant watch over the park. To the park visitors I encountered on hikes who responded to my requests of favorite things about the park, many thanks! Thanks too to the Thurmont Library staff, facilitated by Linda Sundergill and Ranger Carrie, who hosted the nature journal workshop. My deep appreciation to the writers in my writing groups, who always provide invaluable feedback--Saundra, Matt, Anne and Albert; and Michaele, Alex, Lauren and Sarah. Warm hugs to friends who joined me on hikes and cookouts. And to my family, who participated in my residency in so many ways--Annie, who took her father and me camping at Owens Creek

54

Printed in the United States
by Baker & Taylor Publisher Services